Enigma Variations And

by

Paul Roche

Published in 1974
by
The Thornhill Press
7 Russell Street
Gloucester

ISBN 0 904110 11 7

Printed by
Albert E. Smith (Printers) Ltd., Gloucester.

Dedication

for Priscilla Cunningham : a few
images to celebrate the marriage of
a little truth to a little art, and so engender
—I hope—a little entertainment.

Contents

I

Enigma Variations

Note to the Dismayed

Yes, many of these poems (part I) do seem to glory in the enigmatic. I hope this is not mere pretension on my part or, worse, bloody-mindedness. What I wanted was a pattern of language and concepts which wrenched syntax a little to create their own imaginative tension and set up an impetus of words towards perceptions beyond the ordinary use of words. It is all very much an exercise in the poem-as-sound-structure. Read with the ears rather than with the eyes I think the poems can be treated as a sort of hieroglyphic counterpoint (each line a bar) trusted to give out scant meaning except in the act of being played. Otherwise, I apologise for the portentousness. The Rosetta Stone is in the reading.

P.R.

Proem

Everything is against
   the stage scenery :
Boulevards and palaces
   and the perpetually young :
Things incredible
   and centuries away—
A sad and faded perifery
   romantically inhuman.
Yet many costumes, many blossoms
Enrich the equatorial
   conflagrations of history
Wax flowers artificially real
   are hopes that live
We almost believe
   their frightful energy :
Freaks of a fierce
   and elemental humour :
Creation

Alone

It might be the city
In the city of
In which to be
In an empty
Room ; it might be
A staggering—gaunt—
On a stage haunted
By skeletons and bones
With unbreathed words
A something alone
It might be
A weak seedling
A brave flaunting
Like Chatterton dying
In an empty
His poems white birds
Drinking and lilting
Over his bleeding

To One Spent

To one spent
On the streets
Of empty alleluias
Of pot and weed
A tall old man
With a fine white
Stern need
Flowing to help
Offers a retreat
To the heap of self
From needle and speed
Empty cushions
And false savannas
Of arsenic-green
Pink sleep

At Another Time

At another time he would have
He will have he did
Too much and too little
For a warmer climate
Of parrots and camelias
Drop his key and sharply
Think of a nickel
The more his needs, the greater
Too much and too little
And the greater the less
Sleep dreams beams
Of gold noons started
Through his cobwebs his
Ambitious streams then
The lifelong lifting
Of his thin
Reft nets

The Glory of the Inept

Every man and every
To keep his small patch
Pipe and stove and kettle
Or ordering his meal
And coughing a little
Adjusting his and carefully
Watching the waitress
Carefully his tie
Fearing a loosened
Loose fly, shoelace
All undress
And the hollow in his eye
Can never have been
Small but the greatest
Though called timorous
Standing and stiffening
Standing in the mud
Thin against the rain
Yet and yet and yet
This timorous defaulter
Even this failure
Of dishcloth grey O
Will be has been
Saved mud-brave
Wet
Scarecrow

All Things Are Full of Gods (Thales)

I generally manage the violence
(That is
Get by, cope with)
The grass-attacked pavements
Energy of winds ; yes
Generally manage the valley
Needled with slim
Young pines and far
Dereliction of violet
Sad mountains yes
And stalled car—
Generally manage the morning :
Four naked walls
And male brown bare
Feet and the evening
Manage the dregs
Of ballpoint defunct
As old tea generally
Manage but begging
To see, to see
The gods all things
Are full of, even *the*
Billboards. Begging
A pigmy teapot and
A large pinecone
(The teapot neat
Of brass and tin
The cone imbricated
Wooden, overblown)
Manage but begging
O begging and begging
A neat teapot
And a dry
Bristling forest bone

Mercenary Times

They belong to a stiffly hysterical
Chatter of plastic flowers
They belong to those lower
Epicureans who kill time :
The militant supersuds piling
In frothy bastions. Slime
Oilslicks immaculate
With rainbow bloom
A race of crabs scrambling
Up and up the tower
They do not belong to the gem
In you and me and him
Or soul's high noon
Of Xanadu in the grime
Or those epicureans higher
With gold-pan and sieve
Whose very dust is fire
To make time live

The Body Snatcher

His eyes a spade
His brain a casket
His would be slowly
Over the boulders
Into the holy
Cemetery-library :
Pages to loot
Under the idols
Books the tombstones
Under the lunelight
Dead words lively
Under the gloaming
Cerebral worms
Under-turning
The grey-faced slabs

Out of Kelter

The repertory, the litany
Of Prometheus began
Bound gargantuan
To the advertised mountain :
Man's progress, regress
Down, down, clown
Ingress, egress
All things sour
Out of kelter, sweetly
Burning plastics, suddenly
Bowl of milk blighted
Missing teeth biting
Exhausts exhausting
Nostrils curdling
Wire wool scorching
And someone laughing
For somewhere is Scorpio
With prick up searching
Somewhere squashed dollar
O fiery penis
O phallic hosanna :
Searching with a sting

Too Much With Us, Getting And

We are too much
And too many a friend
Without reserve
Supporting a drunkard
Or sleepwalker walking
And now I remember
(Sometimes myself) :
Three girls and a river
And my heart in a mist
And six ways to go
But the puddles were wonder
And the white meadows crowded
And the primroses beside the . . .
If only so many books weren't
And now computers
Weren't such bullies
So the sewage-works only
And the horizon of tower-flats
And a new where the tree was
And dead cars flurrying
Which do not and without any
Are hearses hurrying
Towards more money

Follage (or Fool's Knowledge)

A clot of facts in the brain of a fool
Cloaca, clogging
Collecting and collecting
A midden of knowledge :
Tea leaves, orange pips and bits of gristle
Statistics and the fag ends of principles
Plugging the passage to the sea
Nothing flows
Eyes ears fingers nose
Jammed together, matted
In nests of old hair
Instinct anally stoppered
In the arse-hole of the cerebrum :
The brainbox blocking
Everything the body knows

The Poem as Sound Sword

Phut phut phut a stripling Honda
And the pizzicato of noon crickets
Turn into splinters of ice and glass
Like the tongue-dart of a crushed lemon
Or gush of sherbert in the mouth
Like a pang or shriek
Of ammonia in a sleepy nose . . .
The poem is sword that opens words :
Fruit lanced by the harsh beak
Trembling ice on the pond torn
Thought gashed by a word's sound
As fig bursts with a garnet wound
And images like butterflies
Scatter on the trees and stones—
Words opened in a dream
Seams pierced, scents released
Freshets of sun in a spilt breeze

Inner Spaces

i) HORAE

A nostalgic clamour soddens
the blood as I walk
through these moments, these
ordinary visions, these
trees seen blind, this
apprehension behind
the red brick buildings
and under me this
ordinary ground felt
close to me as memories
after a shower : spreading
sadness and drenching and distance . . . the clarity
of a panorama—disappearing

ii) PERSONA

My irreducible oneness
withdraws
comes down, bends back
watches
arched like a cat
langorously coiled, shaped
to its own inscape
of condensed black smoke :
soft unapprehendable
savage

iii) ACCEDIA

Wild hives of echoes
refuse
to leave the woods for the roads . . .
Their honey is half poisonous and leads
to exquisite tears :
the crooning of shadows
down unimagined
chaparrals

iv) THE NOOSPHERE

The sheer distances inside
burn and shout
with the infinite
uselessness
of measuring light
still arriving
from nebulae within :
an impetus of legends, impulses
from primaeval cells
gyrate and hurl themselves
into the cushions
of this slowly knowing . . .
But the flat daylight tills
the surfaces only
of this flux . . .

Lieing Around Towards the Truth

Words and their incarnations go
Frolicking in choruses
Jigging on the blackboard
Jamming the radios
Crawling out of wordbanks
Lying around
And most of the time
Missing the missed steps down
From clouds to the ground.
So, every hilarious news-shout
That the cannot-both-be-and-not-be
Of the bud and the brick and the bird
Is at last unhidden
And the missing link found
Between bacon-and-eggs and God
Is, by the bullet-headed herd
(Who dig not print-cemetery or midden)
Underfelt to be addle-born, unsound,
Nonsense prone and ninetenthably absurd.

Half a Glass Of

Half a glass of burgundy
And a green grass bank
Half a glass of green grass
And a bank of burgundy
Half a grass bank
And burgundy in a green glass
Half a bank of grass
And a glass of green burgundy
Half a grass of blurgundy
And a green brass blank
Half a glass of clean grease
And a blink of glurgundy
Heelf a brass gleenk
And blurgundy in a grass gleese
Herlf a grease of glank
And a glunk of blast greegundy
Half a bank of grass glass
And a green of glargundy
Half a glass of burgundy
And a green grass bank

II
And

Note to the Sexually Genteel and the . . .

Should you be shocked by some of the words I use, it is no excuse
for me to say " But I never intended it ". Nor would this be true.
And yet I plead motives which I believe are wholesome. One of the
jobs of the poet—besides pleasing and telling the truth—is to arrest
and to wound, provided this can be done with illuminatory impact.
His whole design, surely, is to apprehend being through the power
of his syllables . . . I too am shocked when four-letter words are
used nihilistically or for their own sake.

Should you be outraged, however, by the blatant gallimaufry
(not to say miscegenation) of poems in AND—Sophocles lumped
together with Fruitflies, Teddy bears shoved in with God—I think
you have good reason to be. All I can say is that for me a teddy
bear or a fruitfly, or even a Camelectrosaurus Rex, is ultimately as
theological as great Sophocles himself . . . Be that as it may, I shall
try next time to be poetically more circumspect and aesthetically
more choosy.

P.R.

Post Coital Tristesse

Zeus with his eyebrows of dark blue
A certain shadow in the wine
The hour gone and the sheets remain
A certain shadow in the wine
Zeus with his eyebrows of dark blue

Arethusa in the stream
Flowers floating in the spring
No more blooming : noon gone
Flowers floating in the spring
Arethusa in the stream

So Alphaeus caught his nymph
Fierce chase is now a pond
Already green. Algae grow
Fierce chase is now a pond
So Alphaeus caught his nymph

Zeus with his eyebrows of dark blue
Arethusa in the stream
So Alphaeus caught his nymph
A certain shadow in the wine
Flowers floating in the spring
Fierce chase is now a pond
Zeus with his eyebrows of dark blue

Male and Female
(Soul Knows no Gender)

We meet now as two souls
You are not girl
I am not male

You knew me and I knew you
Only as male
And you as girl

We meet now as two souls
I am not male
You are not girl

What comes to soul never came
When you knew me
And I was male

What came to soul was not the same
When I knew you
And you were girl

You and I were not to blame
For I was male
And you were girl

But now that you are only you
I only I
No girl or male

What comes is real and I can say
We never knew
Until this day

We are two souls you are not girl
I am not male
We are the same

We meet again and now we know
That I am I
And you are you

These Pronouns Can Be Dangerous

I me they he
You her him thee :
Pronouns which are poisonous
If eaten daily
Or in quantity
For they separate the tissues
Cut air from the cells
Dissolve the pan-creative nerve
Make each of the chromosomes
Excessively private
(' Idiotes ' is the Greek)
I me they he
You her him thee :
A chorus, a bacchic dance
A goat caught and killed
A scapegoat ? Young lion ?
It is Pentheus, a person
Made excessively private
(An idiot)
Cut off and killed
By I me they he
You her him thee

Why Didn't Anyone Ever Tell Me ?

Why didn't anyone ever tell me
That every second I am making history ?
Congruent supersuds herd in the washing machine.
The foot pressed on the pedal blurs the scenery.

High frequencies of angels atomize the sky and sea
Into a weft of being without a single seam.
Why didn't anyone ever tell me
That every second I am making history ?

Gullies of rust are putrefying in the chromium cemetery.
Oil climbs up the trees ; the beaches are obscene.
The foot pressed on the pedal blurs the scenery.

The hair of boys and girls falls loosened musically.
Money and megapolice have halitosed their dream.
Why didn't anyone ever tell me
That every second I am making history ?

The missing moments wail the world's great melancholy.
A million miles an atom come to where we've been.
The foot pressed on the pedal blurs the scenery.

The sirens and the billboards scream : hysterical credulity.
Not a sparrow falls nor fades a single jean.
Why didn't anyone ever tell me
That every second I am making history ?
The foot pressed on the gas wipes out the scene.

From My Dorm Window

From my godlike position—
Dammit where's my pencil ?
My godlike position at the window
Of the campus dormitory
Just by the exit
Where I stand still . . .

Ready ?
Blast ! Where's my notebook ? . . . So
Just by the exit
I watch the boys and girls come and go
And it makes me young and old
As I catch their look
Passing.

See ?
There I've netted two
Just in the nick :
Two young men coming in together.
I've got them for a moment moving
Into my cosmology
Before they quit :

One longhaired, in jeans and blue,
One amber with a golden beard.
They jostle metaphysics entire
And every psychedelic trip
In their moon-chipped nude white laughter
As they quip.

Gone. Both. But here's another :
A serious single swinging
Boy with nutbrown down
Loping pensive to the dorm door.
Has he some idea
Of Fate the terrible arranger
Fate the clown ?
Has he—already ?

Another :
Someone's sweetheart, someone's sister,
This time going out : the back of a girl,
Her bare toes running up the grass hide
Of the small hill outside
As her opulent trim haunches swing
And my whole male id
Sacred and profane, in tune
With the atmosphere
Cries :
Tup her tup her have her love her, yes sing
because of the beauty
Of what I see.

I teach them Sophocles and Dante
And how to scan a poem and know
The running rhythm of a rose
The design of chaos
In everything old and new
Everything that grows—

I do, I do.
Oh God may it make them learn
That not a quaesar burns
With more fragrant yearning
Than the sweet quake of their feet
Over the mere dust of what they own.

Make them aware.
I could not bear it to be told
That these young thews and minds were thrown
Into a heap of blind clay
Dull to the glory and the pain
Of juvescence known.

No no ! Not from my window :
Not youth selling nutbrown down and amber,
Toes, buttocks, tupping and gold
And moon-chipped nude white laughter ;
No, not for mere buying and selling
Of indifferent age,
For lobotomized fires
(Eating and sleeping in a convenient way)
—Make them aware, make them aware—
And not the weather reports of the day.

A Song of Being

Everyone is walking with an inner space
Everyone is walking into space
Everyone is walking from and through and to
Everyone is walking into place
Everyone is walking with an inner space.

Everyone is moving with an inner time
Everyone is moving into time
Everyone is moving inside, outside, through
Everyone is moving forward and along
Everyone is moving with an inner time.

Everyone is growing with an inner change
Everyone is growing into change
Everyone is growing inwards, outwards, from
Everyone is growing throughwards and beyond
Everyone is growing with an inner change.

Everyone is being with an inner pace
Everyone is being into being his pace
Everyone is being below, above, beside
Everyone is being before, within, behind
Everyone is being with an inner pace.

Everyone is walking with an inner space
Everyone is moving with an inner time
Everyone is growing with an inner change
Everyone is being with an inner pace
Walking, moving, growing, being
Within, beside, beyond, behind
From and to and in and through
Everyone is growing
Everyone is going
Everyone is coming, coming, coming
Everyone is . . .
Becoming.

The Divine Potency

His river continuously
    pours into moulds
They hold its flowing
    to the moment the moment goes :
Set like a stone his image
    yet soft as a seedling grows
It breathes through a virgin's skin
    or—just as a leaf blows—
Wafts all there is in a flux
    of new into old
Till virgin or leaf, ivy
    or milk-green flow
Are held in a mirror, a fossil
    and then let go
Back to the river in spate
    no virgin or leaf can hold
Where the full cascade is Being
    and being the mold.

Superstition Sometimes

Tealeaves or crystal balls :
Superstition sometimes
Is suddenly a vision
Of what is not yet there :
The hollow in the bowl
Present by its absence
Or like a space between
The sentinels of reason
For the sieged persona.
Superstition sometimes
Is a sudden hole
In the web of fact
Opening on the might be
Through a lens absurdly,
Subliminally focussed
On a peacock's feather
Or the tarot pack.

Philoctetes (2nd Choral Ode)*
(The Chorus of sailors, coming upon the ten-year abandoned
Philoctetes, cannot believe their eyes)

     I heard it said
      but never saw it seen
How Zeus the almighty son of Cronus racked
the body of a man who came to steal
     his own wife from his bed—
     Ixion—on a furious wheel
But neither have I heard nor seen
any fate that can compare
     for black despair
     with this man's here :
Who never hurt a human being
     Made no foes
     A just man to the just—
Yet left like this to decompose

     And now
     (I am amazed)
How did he keep his hold
     day after day
Desolate and alone
With the gride of the combers grounding near . . .
     How :
On such totally tear-marked
     mind-martyred years ?

None but his own next man
     No power to walk and none
even near with whom to talk his pain
     and conjure some support—refrain—
     against the plague that gorged
     his flesh and blood . . .

*Sophocles, lines 676-729

No none, as he crawls
(between the spasms)
like a baby which has lost its nurse
—back and forwards on all fours—
hunting something that will quench his curse
and staunch with healing leaves and cool
from the comforting soil
The trickling boiling sore
that seeps hot gore
from his poisoned heel

He plucks from the pious earth
no root or fruit or seed—
none of that provender we
wrest from the earth with toil
Only his bow
with its fast-feathered arrow can wing
for his body's need
(now and then)
some living thing

Poor lost soul !'
Ten long years
unslaked by a single drop of wine !
Casting around for puddles with his eyes bent low
as he crouches down

But blessed he emerges now
Great through suffering
Because this prince's son
—Neoptolemus—in good time
shall cleave the seas and bring
him home at last :
Home to the Malian naiads
on the river Sperchius' banks
Where high over Oeta's heights
the man with the shield of brass
(Heracles on his pyre)
passed away to the gods
—incandescent passed—
through Zeus's fire

On a Fruitfly Approaching My Wineglass

Shall I tell you, friendly fruitfly,
   pert mouse of the insects,
   flying so spry
   sniffing and bobbing
   in the air nearby,

   how much the divine
dithers through your weaving
towards this claret of mine
where God smells the wine ?

   O vibrant speck,
shall I tell you the treking
of solstars round the sun
deciphers the horizon
no more than your own
   ether pecking ?

Natural Theology

As I got into bed I saw a flea
Hop under the sheets, or so I thought,
Then immediately :
" A part of God is in bed with me . . .
But there are no parts to God at all :
We have him not or we have him whole."

So I did not hunt that flea awhile,
Being in bed with God maybe
Yet wondering still how that could be :
God himself in bed with me
When God himself was not a flea ?

And then I thought : " If I crush this flea
Nothing of God will cease to be
And I'll have no less of God at all
Than when he lets a sparrow fall.
But even everything that's here,
Sheets, pillows, blankets, bed
(Come to think of it, the air)
Are just as much not parts of God
As this insectile animal,
Yet just as much the tangible
Expression of him everywhere :
Not in parts but always whole."

Beyond this thought I could not go.
Therefore with no more ado
I let this flea (if flea it was)
Fulfill his role,
And snuggled down with God and all.

Much-Hugged Teddy-Bears Look Forlorn*

When men and women love they don't look worn
(A trickle of sawdust is the saddest sign)
But much-hugged teddy bears look forlorn :

Frayed faces, napless as an August lawn,
Bluebottles buzzing round the windowpane,
Yet men and women love and don't look worn.

A wooden heart bleeds sawdust when it's sawn.
Stuffed with the past a soft heart flows like wine
And much-hugged teddy bears look forlorn

Though warm and bracken-hearted as a faun . . .
Crumpets and eggs for tea—the beat of the rain—
Men and women love and don't look worn.

If no bullseyes hot as peppercorn
And no stroking makes a human pine
Much-hugged teddy bears look forlorn.

Plumcake pupils popping like a prawn
Of teddies old enough to drink champagne
Make men and women love and not look worn.

The dial on the kitchen clock can wear a shine
And sunbeams shoot straight through the dullest brain
When much-hugged teddy bears look forlorn
And men and women love and don't look worn.

*for Napier and Herck : a very old and
  a middleaged teddy bear.

The Sun Grazing

The mist-eating sun
Was on his third course :
His hors d'oeuvres the dew
On cold blades of grass
His entrée twelve clouds
Sautéed in blue
And now his dessert
From the noon where he browsed
Was the cream of three seas
Coddled in spume.

The Camelectrosaurus Rex

It is dangerous to be in the room alone with it.
I was in the room alone with it at dusk.
The plates along the studio wall were winking dim.
The gasfire smouldered quietly in the room,
Playing along my nails and fingertips.
The Camelectrosaurus Rex had stood all day
On its spider-easle legs as dead as sticks ;
The oblong of its mouth (or was it Cyclops eye ?)
Rectangular and bland, opaque and blind :
A small latescent window with a vacuous stare.
Yet when I looked towards the skylight where it loomed
Against the twilight of an empty street,
Some fraction of an alteration in its stance
Made me stir : uneasily and suddenly alone.
I wished a goldfish or canary in the room,
Something living to redress a presence there.
I thought I heard a ticking noise. I shivered.
The Camelectrosaurus Rex's smaller eye
(Or was it ear ?) began, I thought, to tinge
With a dull anaemic dawn as green as phlegm
Flickering and swimming through its retina.
I thought of jelly setting in an embryo :
A dead unfocussed spot congealing to an eye,
Or as if amoebas teemed electronically therein.
Did machine turn plant and plant turn conscious thing ?
Did heart and brain and plan somewhere switch on ?
The Camelectrosaurus Rex was watching me.
" Dumb robot, tree of lenses, nubs and wires,
I'll soon have you unplugged," I said and took a stride.
Whereupon, the box-head jerked—or so it seemed—
And angled, sinister, towards a socket
As if it challenged me to race it to the switch.
I reached—and now there could be no mistake—
As I hit against a twiggy limb
A stick-arm reared and in a leech-like clamp
(Or poisoned limpet's) shot my arm with pain.
A squirm of flex—one tentacle and then another—
Licked out like cobras from the creature's belly,

Swelling and swirling as its veins began to glow.
My every touch was trapped in viscous webs
Which clung to my flesh. I could not drag away.
Nothing that I fingered but it triggered
Currents of venom which rinsed me through with stings.
The Camelectrosaurus Rex was now ablaze :
Heat and pressure screaming purple in its head.
Every wire was live and raced and hissed
And swole along my arms, my eyes, my brain.
Like a giant anemone it magnetized me in.
Its needle kisses singing and sucked me to the bone.

Not till the morning did they find me there,
The Camelectrosaurus Rex astraddle me :
My body prone and charred, my hands a mummy's.
The gasfire smouldered quietly in the room,
Gently playing along my mummy's hair.
The Camelectrosaurus Rex stood by skylight still
On its spider-easel legs as dead as sticks,
The oblong of its mouth and Cyclops eye
Rectangular and bland, opaque and blind :
A small latescent window with a vacuous stare.

Nobody believed me—what my body said—
" It is dangerous to be in the room alone with it."

Sovereign Simplicity

I face the everlasting fact I am a being alone
And that which is alone and one with me
Is that which I must share with all
As fodder always for my being other :
My kisses, pain, recalcitrance . . .
All those conditions for my being at all,
My brotherhood with stones and trees
With stars animals and souls
Even my subliminal and filial
Contingency on God,
I make other and my own :
Assimilate into the alone.
My soul and body
Go out grazing in a team
Digesting everything I know and am
Into a sole territory, person, king :
Irreducibly its own
Because it is not everything.